HISTORIC PHOTOS OF
DALLAS
IN THE 50s, 60s, AND 70s

TEXT AND CAPTIONS BY RUSTY WILLIAMS

TURNER
PUBLISHING COMPANY

The Dallas skyline is about to undergo a transformation. In this 1950s photo, looking southward from Munger Street (now Woodall Rogers Freeway), the Republic Bank and Mercantile and Magnolia (Mobil) buildings dominate downtown. A decade later, these buildings would be dwarfed by others.

HISTORIC PHOTOS OF
DALLAS
IN THE 50s, 60s, AND 70s

Turner Publishing Company
200 4th Avenue North • Suite 950
Nashville, Tennessee 37219
(615) 255-2665

www.turnerpublishing.com

Historic Photos of Dallas in the 50s, 60s, and 70s

Copyright © 2010 Turner Publishing Company

Library of Congress Control Number: 2010926750

ISBN: 978-1-59652-742-3

Printed in China

10 11 12 13 14 15 16 17—0 9 8 7 6 5 4 3 2 1

Contents

Suburban growth in the 1960s stretched city services, forcing renovation and expansion of many city facilities. When the East Dallas (Lakewood) branch of the Dallas Public Library was closed for remodeling in 1961, librarians organized a sidewalk "Carnival of Books" to serve their patrons. Books were dispensed from stalls, library windows, and "two-legged bookmobiles" until construction was complete.

Acknowledgments

This volume, *Historic Photos of Dallas in the 50s, 60s, and 70s,* is the result of the cooperation and efforts of many individuals, organizations, and corporations. It is with great thanks that we acknowledge the valuable contribution of the following for their generous support:

The Dallas Public Library
The Library of Congress

―――――――――

With the exception of touching up imperfections that have accrued over time and cropping where necessary, no changes have been made to the photographs. The focus and clarity of many photographs is limited to the technology and the ability of the photographer at the time they were taken.

PREFACE

In the space of three decades, Dallas grew from the plucky, black-land prairie town of "Big D (My, Oh Yes!)" to the Dallas of *Dallas.*

Like Atlanta, Seattle, Kansas City, or Denver—all cities with about the same population—Dallas in 1950 was a proud, ambitious town of some regional importance. All these mid-tier cities expected growth from WWII veterans who chose to leave farms for factory jobs in the cities, and all hoped to reap a harvest of young men educated on the G.I. Bill who might be counted on to start and run profitable businesses.

But 30 years later, Dallas was a top-tier city, an international city, and the others weren't. By whatever measure you choose—population growth, building permits, bank deposits, housing starts, or number of Jujubes sold at local movie theaters—Dallas doubled the growth of those other cities.

It wasn't just a matter of size. By the end of the 1970s, Dallas exerted a cultural influence far beyond its ranking as the seventh largest city in the nation. Dallas was home to "America's Team," a pro football team whose silver star was as recognizable to a goatherd in Norway as to a fan in Paducah. Dallas drove the fashion market for Sunbelt cities, and Tokyo teens emulated the big hair and just-so makeup that every Dallas debutante learns in kindergarten. Executives carrying briefcases stuffed with important papers arrived and departed hourly from Dallas's international airport for oil and finance centers around the globe.

In 1950, Dallas was a comfortable stopover at the intersection of three major rail lines for passengers on their way to Cleveland or St. Louis or Chicago. Three decades later Dallas was an Oz, a glittering emerald city on the horizon where glamorous and important people lived while doing fascinating things.

This book provides nearly two hundred glimpses of Dallas in the 1950s, 1960s, and 1970s. You'll see the cop on the corner, the kids in school, the crowd at the ball park. If you're of a certain age, you'll remember buildings that are now long gone, parades passed by, or days you'd as soon forget. If you didn't live in Dallas during those decades, you may marvel at how quaint—how usual—life seemed to be in a city that was charging into the future like a rodeo bull leaving his stall. Whatever your perspective, as you flip from page to page, you'll see a city in the process of transforming its skyline, its roads, its civic institutions, its public behavior, and its sense of self and worth.

You may not see the definitive "why" between the covers of this book. Turn the pages and stare at the bunting over the Cotton Bowl Parade route; it won't tell you how Dallas built a national reputation in pro sports. Get out your magnifying glass to examine a building's stonework, and you won't learn why the structure was built in the first place. Look through the window into the faces of trolley-car passengers, but don't expect to learn why they chose to live and work in Dallas. These images and these words won't tell you why Dallas grew from the prairie town of "Big D (My, Oh Yes!)" to the Dallas of *Dallas* in the span of just 30 years.

But the pictures will give you some pretty good clues.

—*Rusty Williams*

In 1950 Dallas is ready to stretch its legs and grow. In this northward view, a partially complete Central Expressway curves away toward the horizon. In just three decades the city's population would double, and the skyline would be virtually unrecognizable.

THE 1950s: "BIG D (MY, OH, YES!)"

You're from Big D—I can guess,
By the way you drawl and the way you dress.

Dallas in the fifties had its own song. It was a national hit, a clever little show tune that came from a barely remembered Frank Loesser Broadway musical. Jo Stafford and a half-dozen others put it on vinyl, and you'd hear the song everywhere— on the radio, on jukeboxes, sung weekly on *Your Hit Parade.* Tell the piano-bar guy at the Drake Hotel in Chicago that you were from Dallas, and he'd bang out "Big D (My, Oh, Yes)." Meet another vacationing family at the tourist court in New Mexico, and next thing you know, all the kids would be singing "Big D" around the pool.

The song was a lot like Dallas itself: self-referential, self-deprecating, and comfortable once you got to know it. Outsiders came to see that Big D wasn't typically Texas, with its flash and brag and more money than sense. Instead, Big D was self-aware; it had a sense of humor; it had a hint of the cosmopolitan.

Don't it give you pleasure to confess
That you're from Big D? My, oh, yes!

It's too much of a stretch to claim that a show tune could turn a town into a city. But as Big D went about the work of the fifties—attracting workers from colleges and farms, building homes and schools for their families, paving the roads they needed, and organizing fairs and parades to entertain them—the people of Dallas did so with an extra element of pride and a sense of self-confidence that other towns may have lacked.

When historians discuss the transformation of Dallas that began in the 1950s, they credit the city's civic leadership, insightful bankers, forward-thinking educators, and benevolent rich people. That may be so. But it's a safe bet that every one of those folks (and the historians, too) learned to spell the name of their city with a Big "D"-little "a"-double "l"-"a"-"s."

Visitors stroll the Midway during the 1950 State Fair of Texas. They may have enjoyed a traditional corn dog or visited any of the thirty-six sideshow attractions. The more adventuresome may have ridden the Rock-O-Plane, the Sky Wheel, or the Comet Coaster.

Dallas owed its growth in the early part of the century to being at the center of a rail network that moved goods and passengers across the state and nation. Here, a mariachi band serenades passengers departing on an MKT (Missouri-Kansas-Texas Railroad) train for San Antonio.

Policing in Dallas in the 1950s included traffic control at busy intersections, such as this one at Main and Harwood Street (looking north) outside the White Plaza Hotel.

A. Harris & Co. grew from a small dry-goods store in 1887 to one of Dallas's nameplate department stores. The company moved to this location at the corner of Main and Akard streets in 1914.

Even a dusting of snow can befuddle Dallas drivers. Here, drivers navigate a tricky railway underpass to enter the downtown area.

Freezing rain, ice, and snow from a vicious 1951 storm bring crosstown city traffic to a halt. This view looks north on Akard Street from Main Street. Walgreen Drugs advertises one-day film developing on its window—"In by 9, out by 5."

The popularity and prowess of Southern Methodist University football players such as Doak Walker, Kyle Rote, and Fred Benners earned Dallas a national reputation as a football town in the early 1950s. Though the team moved into the Cotton Bowl for regular games in 1947, they pose for this team photo on the SMU campus.

In the postwar years, small manufacturing and food-processing plants proliferated throughout Dallas County. Even a small plant, such as this cannery at 2822 Glenfield Street, could pump $3 million a year into the Dallas economy.

Elm Street glitters in this time exposure, looking east from around Field Street. Downtown Dallas offered late-night shopping, dining, and entertainment most nights of the week.

For Texans new to city-living in Dallas, rodeo was still an essential entertainment, and small arenas surrounded the city. The Audie Murphy Rodeo Arena, east of Euless on Highway 183, was named after the popular Texas war hero and movie star.

The small community of Mesquite in Southeast Dallas County gained national attention with the Mesquite Championship Rodeo, founded in 1958. In 1993, the Texas Legislature declared Mesquite the Rodeo Capital of Texas.

Robert E. Fulton's *Airphibian* could have been the perfect Dallas vehicle: drive the car over city streets, or strap on the detachable wing-and-tail section for a smooth flight to distant Texas towns. Despite this publicity visit to Dallas in 1951, Fulton's roadable aircraft never took off with the general public.

In 1947 the *Texas Special* was upgraded to a diesel-powered streamliner, providing 24-hour direct service between San Antonio and St. Louis. The 14-car train—identifiable by its bright red aluminum side panels—was equipped with seven sleeper cars, three coaches, an observation car, a lounge car, and this luxurious dining car. The last *Texas Special* ran in 1965.

Despite polio fears that threatened to close all city swimming pools in the early 1950s, Dallas continued with plans to complete new pools in Samuell Park and Weiss Park by summer 1953. All neighborhood pools were racially segregated, but in two cases that year the U. S. Supreme Court signaled that segregation of municipal recreation facilities would soon come to an end.

The view west on Elm Street (from near Harwood) shows an active retail district. Down the block to the left is Titche-Goettinger, another of Dallas's nameplate department stores. To the right are the Majestic, Melba, and Tower theaters. (The Majestic interspersed live stage acts with movies.)

The expansive lawn in front of Dallas Country Club was an ideal location for a traditional Easter Sunday egg hunt. From its turn-of-the-century beginnings as a golfing club for men, Dallas Country Club was, by the 1950s, the center of Dallas's exclusive social circuit.

A stiff breeze on Sunday afternoon, October 21, 1951, fanned a fire that destroyed six businesses and a half block of downtown Dallas in the 1600 block of Main Street (near Stone Street). Firemen later speculated that the fire was caused by improper disposal of smoking materials inside Manuel's Tailors, located above National Shirt Shops.

This view of the "Akard Street Canyon" (looking northward from Commerce Street) shows why this was one of the busiest areas of downtown Dallas in the fifties. The Adolphus Hotel, stopover for movie stars and oil millionaires, is at left; the Magnolia Building, headquarters of Magnolia Petroleum Company (later Mobil Oil) is on the right.

Dallas Mayor R. L. Thornton greets United States Senator Lyndon Johnson in a room at the Baker
Hotel in 1952. Johnson was in Dallas that October to ride in the State Fair of Texas parade and cut
the ribbon that opened the gates to the fair for its 15-day run.

The Gainesville Community Circus (including Gerry, the performing baby elephant, and an ice-skating clown troupe) performed in front of the Melba Theater for the opening of Cecil B. DeMille's movie *The Greatest Show on Earth* in 1952.

Golfing legend Ben Hogan was the defending champion and odds-on favorite when he came to Dallas for the 52nd U.S. Open golf tournament at Northwood Country Club in 1952. Hogan led the tournament going into the final day, but dark horse Julius Boros took home the $4,000 top prize.

Popular WWII general and newly minted Republican Dwight D. Eisenhower brought his presidential campaign to Dallas several times in 1952, drawing larger crowds each time. When more than 6,000 people showed up for an early morning stopover in October, Ike and wife Mamie were forced to address the crowd from atop the marquee on the west end of Union Station.

In 1952 R. W. Burnett, owner and president of the Texas League Dallas Eagles, announced he would breach the color line and hire black baseball players, the first league team to do so. Here, new pitcher-outfielder Dave Hoskins signs autographs for a largely black crowd, probably at Burnett Field in Oak Cliff.

The Dallas Eagles won three Texas League pennants and the Dixie Series trophy in the early 1950s. A tireless promoter, team owner R. W. Burnett brought exciting minor league baseball to the area while trying to secure a major league franchise for Dallas.

Texas textile manufacturer Giles Miller brought national league football to Dallas in 1952 when he acquired the New York Yanks and renamed them the Dallas Texans. Miller considered SMU's Matty Bell, Sammy Baugh, Curly Lambeau, and even Bear Bryant, but the head coaching job went to Jimmy Phelan. Season tickets were $21.60 for six home games in the Cotton Bowl; sideline seats were $3.60. Here, they are playing the San Francisco 49ers.

Springtime was athletic trophy time at the Hockaday School. Founded in 1913 by Miss Ela Hockaday, the school had a reputation for providing an excellent education for young women. These women show off trophies awarded for tennis, swimming, and other sports. By the end of the decade, the Hockaday School would move from their original location on Greenville Avenue to a larger campus on Forest Lane in far North Dallas.

A mock atomic bomb drill at all Dallas public schools in 1953 tested preparedness for nuclear attack. These students at Maple Lawn Elementary were taught to drop to their hands and knees with faces to the floor at the first sound of alarm sirens. The drills continued in public schools throughout the 1950s.

Dallas-born Air Force leader Lieutenant General Charles P. Cabell was on hand to inspect the military equipment, servicemen, and ROTC bands that made up this Armed Forces Day parade in 1953. In this photo, the parade is moving eastward on Main Street as it crosses Ervay Street.

Dallas was an enthusiastic movie-going town, and studios often arranged for their stars to visit for personal appearances. In 1953, members of the international cast of Paramount's *Pleasure Island* spend a spring afternoon by the lagoon at Fair Park.

In 1947, Fort Worth contracted to build an airport intended to serve Fort Worth and Dallas air passengers. The Greater Fort Worth International Airport (Amon Carter Field) opened in 1953 and was located halfway between the two cities. The "Airport of Tomorrow" was equipped to handle the jet airliners then coming into service. Dallas travelers refused to abandon Love Field, however, and the costly new airport was mostly abandoned in the 1960s.

In 1920 half of all Texans earned their living on a farm; by 1950 eight out of ten Texans lived in towns and cities. One of the few places in Dallas to find peaches, tomatoes, watermelons, squash, and other produce straight from the farm was at Dallas Farmers Market. Then, as now, farmers would arrive before dawn, bringing garden crops to sell from the backs of their trucks.

A mass of youngsters from farms and small towns of Texas helped set a one-day attendance record of almost 300,000 at the State Fair of Texas on Rural Youth Day, October 10, 1953. Kids and grown-ups came to see Big Tex "talk" for the first time, watch the Ice Cycle arena show, and sneak a peek at the Transparent Man on display at the Dallas Health Museum.

Dallas suffered drought conditions through the the mid-1950s, but dry weather made for abundant cotton crops. At least one farmer had enough raw cotton to let children play in a wagonload of the unprocessed crop before dropping it at the gin.

SMU football players board the Braniff Airways DC-9 that will fly them to South Bend for their game with Notre Dame in 1953. Captain C. V. Carleton, Braniff flight operations manager, piloted SMU's football players on their long away-game trips from 1947 to 1963.

Christmas decorations are replaced by banners welcoming out-of-towners to the Cotton Bowl festivities. Lower Elm Street (looking east from about Griffin Street) was a favorite area for less-affluent shoppers. There were diners, small clubs, dark bars, and Seymour's Credit Clothing, where a man could buy a new suit of clothes for eight dollars and snap-brim hat for a buck.

Even the horse wears a garter in this publicity shot marking the arrival of Hollywood stars for the 1954 Texas premiere of Paramount's *Red Garters*. Left to right are stars Gene Barry, Buddy Ebsen, Guy Mitchell, and Pat Crowley, and Dallas Interstate Theaters manager James O. Cherry. Despite the publicity, Dallas moviegoers failed to appreciate this Broadway-musical-style Western satire.

Lunchtime gawkers on Main Street watch construction of the new Corrigan Building, near Main and Akard. Dallas's 1954 building boom set a city record, with $142.6 million worth of construction authorized by permits, placing the city in the top half dozen of cities in the nation regarding construction costs. Downtown construction and expansion accounted for much of the activity, but single-family home construction in 1954 reached near-record levels as well.

Under the supervision of a Federal Reserve Bank official, a worker incinerates worn-out silver certificates after the currency has been withdrawn from circulation. The Federal Reserve Bank branch in Dallas monitored local banking, aiding in the city's growth as a financial center of the Southwest.

This short section of Elm Street was Dallas's "Theater Row" in the 1950s. The Capitol specialized in Westerns and kids' movies; the Rialto was a first-run house, slightly past its prime. The Palace's huge organ rose from the auditorium floor for concerts between features; the Tower booked sophisticated first-run movies. Only the Majestic survived into the 1970s and is operated as a legitimate theater today.

By 1954, planning was underway to revamp 96 acres south of downtown by building a civic auditorium and eventually a convention center to attract national conventions and meetings. This view, looking west on Marilla Street from Akard, shows buildings that would soon be demolished to build Pioneer Plaza, the auditorium, and the convention center complex.

The intersection of Commerce and Akard streets was known in the 1950s as "the Crossroads of Dallas," with the Adolphus Hotel, Magnolia Building, and Baker Hotel anchoring three of the corners. This view, looking east on Commerce from Akard, shows the Baker Hotel, a favorite of conventioneers, politicians, and partygoers.

A Dallas Railway & Terminal Company streetcar runs southbound on St. Paul Street, approaching Main Street near the entrance to Titche-Goettinger. Streetcars (or "trolleys" or "trolley buses") were the primary form of mass transit in Dallas in the early 1950s, but they would be gone by the end of the decade.

Renovation in downtown Dallas took a tragic turn on Wednesday evening, June 1, 1955, when an old building on Elm Street near Akard collapsed, killing five people, trapping ten, and injuring dozens more. The three-story building was in the process of demolition when it fell into another building housing a tavern and music store. Bystanders wait for news of victims trapped in the rubble.

Volunteers and emergency personnel worked all night to free victims trapped in the collapsed building rubble at Elm Street near Akard. Recovery efforts were hindered by downed live electrical wires and gas seeping into the tangle of brick and beams. The final victim was not recovered until five days later.

Fifteen hundred coonskin-capped youngsters welcomed "Davy Crockett" to Dallas when their hero arrived at Love Field in 1955; thousands more flocked to the Majestic Theater for live stage appearances by actors Fess Parker and Buddy Ebsen and the opening of Walt Disney's *Davy Crockett, King of the Wild Frontier.*

49

Homeward-bound traffic flows smoothly along Central Expressway in this view, looking south toward downtown from the Haskell Street overpass. By 1955 the completed high-speed expressway extended 14 miles, from Live Oak Street to near Campbell Road. Engineers speculated that Central Expressway might one day reach all the way to McKinney.

The appearance of a real-life Texas hero brought more crowds to the Majestic Theater in August 1955 when Audie Murphy came to Dallas for the opening of his autobiographical movie, *To Hell and Back.* Murphy, a native of Greenville, Texas, and WWII hero, admires a stature presented by sculptor Julian Bowles on opening night.

"Little Miss Sunbeam," the dimply spokeskid for Holsum Bread, invited every youngster in Dallas to celebrate her birthday with a party at Fair Park Midway in 1955. These youngsters (and 7,000 more) enjoyed the Midway's thrill rides and other attractions all day, courtesy of the bakery.

Motorcycle outriders clear the way for units of the 1955 State Fair of Texas parade, held on Friday afternoon instead of the usual Saturday morning. A Friday parade was planned to help avoid traffic congestion at the next day's Texas-Oklahoma football contest. The view is west on Main Street toward the Harwood Street intersection.

From beneath the new aluminum awning of the Baker Hotel entrance, the Aldolfus Hotel is catercorner across Commerce and Akard streets. The two hotels hosted most of the famous visitors to Dallas through the early 1950s.

Motorman L. N. Ramsey pilots Dallas's last trolley car as it makes a final run to the car barn on January 14, 1956. A fixture on Dallas streets since 1872, railed trolley transit was considered too inflexible and too old-fashioned for a growing, modern Dallas. The Dallas Railway & Terminal Company retired the electric trolley cars with a fleet of 56 diesel- and gasoline-powered buses.

A new type of transit was unveiled at Fair Park in 1956 when the *Trailblazer* Monorail became fully operational. Intended as a prototype for an extended system, the monorail was plagued by construction and operating delays. Visitors to Fair Park could ride the 1600-foot route for 25 cents, but interest waned, and the *Trailblazer* was removed in 1963.

Originally opened in 1949 to serve white audiences, the 1,500-seat Forest Theater was closed, then
reopened in 1956 as the South's largest theater for blacks only. The grand reopening did turnaway business
with a double bill that included *Helen of Troy* and the *Nat King Cole Story*. John D. Rice, president of
Dallas's Negro Chamber of Commerce, thanked Interstate Theaters for "helping extend the recreational
facilities of his people."

Downtown Dallas traffic was facing gridlock in 1956, and city engineers focused on two troublesome intersections: Canton and Young streets at Harwood. (The view here is east on Young Street.) Purchase of small plots of land from the Scottish Rite Cathedral and Masonic Temple allowed for rerouting the intersections and a (temporary) reduction of traffic tie-ups.

Dallas's spreading population increased the demand for suburban movie theaters. The Wilshire Theater, located on Mockingbird Lane at Skillman Street, celebrated its eleventh anniversary with a neighborhood carnival and street dance in June 1956. Jim Boyd and his band headlined the parking lot entertainment.

Despite the towering presence of Pegasus atop the Magnolia Building and the nearby Adolphus Hotel, lower Commerce Street (looking east from about Austin Street) looks a little down-at-heel. Many of the apparel-sales-rep firms kept offices there in the older buildings, left and right. Once a respectable place for tourists, by 1956 the Hotel Whitmore was home to permanent residents and traveling salesmen on tight budgets.

The State Fair of Texas celebrated its Diamond Jubilee in 1956, and this photo captures much of the essence of those 75 years. Miniature stern-wheelers *Dixie Bell* and *Ole Miss* take passengers on a leisurely cruise around the lagoon while other fairgoers wait at the monorail station for a speedy trip across the length of the grounds. In the background, the Cotton Bowl beckons fairgoers to some of the finest football in the nation.

Following Spread: Springtime clouds float over Dallas in this view looking northeast from around Market and Wood streets. Many of the buildings in the foreground would be demolished in coming years for construction of the convention center complex.

Two of the largest banks in Texas sit side by side on this block of Main Street looking south from Akard. First National Bank (1407 Main) was adjacent to Republic National Bank (1309 Main), but by 1957, Republic had moved into a new building, and the building at 1309 Main was then known as the Davis Building.

The business section of Oak Cliff's Jefferson Boulevard received a makeover in 1957, as seen in this view looking west from Zang Boulevard. Streetcar poles and wires were removed, the street was made into a divided trafficway, and fluorescent lighting was placed along the median strip. The beautification extended from Fifth Street to Willomet Street, a distance of almost two miles.

This blue Fairlane 500 town sedan was "Made in Texas By Texans," according to the sticker placed in its rear window, and it was the two millionth automobile to roll off the line of Dallas's Ford Assembly Plant on April 23, 1957. Ford opened its first full Dallas assembly plant in 1915 at Canton and Williams streets before moving into this facility at 5200 E. Grand in 1925.

Spectators watch the progress of a tornado as it skips through West and Northwest Dallas on April 2, 1957, leaving ten dead and 170 hospitalized. Visible from most parts of the city (and seen here from the 2800 block of Live Oak), the twister first touched down at Cedar Hill, then danced its way northward across Oak Cliff, down the Trinity River levees to just west of Love Field.

The 1957 tornado arrived "with the roar of a thousand freight trains," said a customer at this flattened market in the 1600 block of Singleton. Witnesses along the path of the twister described a black wall of debris moving slowly northward at eight miles an hour. The tornado cut a path of destruction a mile wide and almost 20 miles long, leaving hundreds homeless.

This photo, looking east on Northwest Highway from Douglas Avenue, shows an intersection that was fast becoming part of the city's most active suburban shopping area. Preston Center (out of frame at right) was home to the first suburban Neiman Marcus and Sanger's stores. Shoppers could lunch at Youngblood's Chicken or service their autos at the six-bay Mobil station. The new sanctuary of Park Cities Baptist Church is in the distance.

Other shopping centers provided a convenient alternative for suburban residents who wanted to avoid the long drive into downtown Dallas. When the 45-acre Lochwood Village opened in August 1957 at the intersection of Garland and Jupiter roads, it promised 50 stores (all with air conditioning), free parking for up to 4,000 automobiles, and soft "moonlight" mercury-vapor lighting for safe evening shopping.

Dallas's nighttime skyline glows in this time exposure facing west on Live Oak Street near Cantegral Street. Building slowed somewhat in downtown Dallas in 1957, but workers had already broken ground on the Southland Hotel and Southland Center.

Like downtown retailers, downtown Dallas theaters struggled to hold on to an increasingly suburban clientele. Here, some 40 members of the "Earth Angels," a Dallas motorcycle club, show up for the Rialto Theater's run of two exploitation flicks, *Motorcycle Gang* and *Sorority Girl,* in 1958.

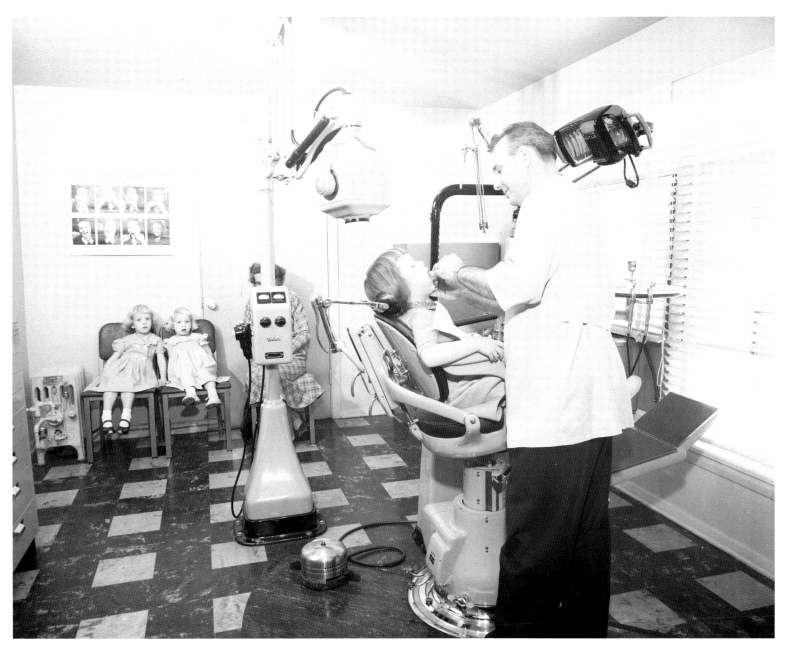

Two apprehensive little girls wait their turn for treatment at the Oak Cliff Lions Club Dental Clinic, which opened in March 1958. Local civic groups were increasingly contributing time and money to the care of Dallas's needy.

Promoters for the movie *Onionhead*, starring Andy Griffith and Walter Matthau, enlisted Dallas boys to perform random good deeds at locations around Dallas. The boys would be rewarded with passes to the movie, which opened in 1958 at the Majestic.

Dallas has plenty of room to spread out, as shown in this view southwestward, along Rock Island Road. Within a few years, a spaghetti-like freeway interchange and small industrial businesses would fill this open space.

Construction crane operator Robert Hall enjoys a one-of-a-kind view of Dallas from his perch atop Southland Center in 1958. At 42 stories, the building would, for a brief time, be the tallest building west of the Mississippi River.

To compete on a national level, Dallas spent $7 million on its new Memorial Auditorium, completed in 1957. The mammoth arena was said to have had a seating capacity of 10,000 and more than 100,000 square feet of exhibit space for conventions and trade shows, and it put Dallas in the topmost bracket of convention cities.

The Dallas Museum of Fine Arts opened in this picturesque location by the Fair Park lagoon in 1936, but the building's limited size (and political considerations) required that much of the museum's collection be kept in storage in the 1950s. In 1955 the Dallas County Patriotic Council charged the museum with exhibiting works by artists with Communist leanings, resulting in the withdrawal of works by Picasso, Diego Rivera, and other politically suspect artists.

In this view looking east from Akard Street, the venerable Mercantile Bank Building towers over Commerce Street. To the left is Sol's Turf Bar and Neiman Marcus; to the right is the Baker Hotel entrance and Steak House Unique.

Main Street (seen here, looking west from St. Paul Street) is decked out in its Christmas finery in 1958. Families would flock to downtown Dallas for the ceremonial lighting of decorations and the annual Christmas parade, which included themed floats, high-school marching bands, drill teams, and, of course, Santa Claus.

Honest Joe's was a Deep Ellum mainstay for more than 40 years, and the store grew to cover almost the entire 2600 block of Elm Street. "Joe"—whose name was actually Rubin Goldstein—said he once loaned $100 on a diamond ring six times in one night as a sidewalk crapshooter found his dice running hot and cold during the evening.

Fires of suspicious origins destroyed two rooming houses in Oak Cliff in February 1959, leaving one dead and dozens injured. Both rooming houses, located just blocks apart, were fully engulfed in smoke and flame when fire crews arrived. The fires left 20 to 30 persons homeless, and caused more than $40,000 damage.

By 1959 so many tall buildings were on the drawing board for downtown Dallas that the 30-story Mayflower Building barely drew interest. The building, located on Akard Street at Pacific Avenue, is under construction in this southward view on Akard Street from San Jacinto Street.

The 12,000 attendees at the Kiwanis International Convention in 1959 who packed Dallas's new convention center arena accounted for just a fraction of the 462,000 visitors brought to the city by conventions, sales meetings, and trade markets that year. By the end of the decade, Dallas was hosting 75 national conventions a year worth more than $62 million to the local economy.

THE 1960s: DEFINING DALLAS

Dallas defined itself in the sixties.

Despite the enthusiasm and growth of the previous decade, Dallas in 1960 still had its roots planted in conservative Southern soil. Dallas schools, businesses, and neighborhoods were racially segregated. White men would appear in photos in the newspapers' business sections, black men would appear in the crime news, and Mexican-Americans were invisible. Blue laws prevented a woman from buying cosmetics on Sunday; local liquor laws prohibited a couple from enjoying a martini at their favorite restaurant. Somehow, Dallas found a way to transcend its Southern lineage in a manner more graceful than many other communities of the time.

Worrisome, too, was a high-decibel political faction that refused to distinguish between liberals, socialists, and Communists, tarring them all with the same broad brush. Venom flowed from that small faction in the early years of the decade until a murder in November 1963 led Dallas to contemplate the effect of extremism on the city's standing and growth.

Dallas weathered the tie-dyed sixties about as well as other cities of the same size. The city tolerated the sit-ins, the protests, the counterprotests, the love-ins, the be-ins, and the festivals that made the period such a passionate time for those who lived through it (and a sideshow for those who didn't).

Then there were the sports. College football in the Cotton Bowl had been around for years, but professional sports blossomed in the 1960s, with minor league baseball, basketball, and hockey teams, and a fairgrounds rivalry between two pro football teams. The teams provided affordable family entertainment and national bragging rights.

Meanwhile, Dallas companies earned a pretty penny manufacturing materiel for an Asian war that was beginning to boil. The money went into banks, and the banks put the money into buildings. Tall buildings. Republic National, Texas Bank, National Bank of Commerce, and First National each added to the skyline during the decade, further defining the look and feel of Big D.

By the end of the decade—with plans for a new city hall, a new courthouse, and more tall buildings on the drawing board—Dallas was beginning to appreciate just how distinctive it was.

Crews prepare the new American Airlines Lockheed Electra for departure from Love Field. Turboprop service, followed soon after by full jet service with Boeing 707s, cut air travel time between Dallas and other major cities by half. In the 1950s, railroads delivered passengers to Chicago in 30 hours; the Lockheed flight took just two.

Sheathed in anodized aluminum panels embossed with the bank's logo, the Republic National Bank building was the tallest in Dallas from 1954 to 1959. The 150-foot tower atop the building had a revolving beacon that shone at night, but complaints from pilots landing at Love Field forced building management to turn it off. This view is east along Pacific Avenue from Akard Street.

Presentation of debutantes at Dallas's annual Idlewild Ball was a tradition that stretched back to the 1880s. But tradition was shattered like fine crystal when the ball moved from the venerable Baker Hotel (its home for a quarter century) to the new Sheraton-Dallas Hotel.

Spring days brought out the sailboats on White Rock Lake. The sport of sailing was made more popular by the introduction of a one-person, 16-foot fiberglass sailing craft. The Corinthian Sailing Club organized regattas and racing series, which were held most weekends throughout the spring-to-fall boating season.

As the war in Vietnam began to simmer, the Dallas–Fort Worth area became a major supplier of war materiel. During the 1960s, Bell Helicopter would sign contracts worth more than $400 million with different branches of the U.S. Armed Forces for its popular *Iroquois* helicopters. Here, a pilot tests the HU-1B intended for use in Southeast Asia by the U.S. Army.

Texans voted Republican in the presidential elections of 1952 and 1956, but Senator Lyndon B. Johnson, running mate of John F. Kennedy, was determined to win the state in 1960. Johnson's visit to Dallas just before Election Day started with enthusiastic crowds, but he and his wife were mobbed, jeered, and threatened by Dallas conservatives (including a Republican congressman) during a lunchtime stroll downtown. It was the first of several events that would earn for Dallas the unfortunate nickname "City of Hate."

When it opened in 1959, Big Town was the Southwest's first enclosed and air-conditioned shopping mall, a futuristic "City of Shops." Advertised as a "family friendly shopping experience," Big Town boasted a cartoon theater for kids and vending machines for snacks and drinks. In the 1960s, however, customers and tenants would largely abandon Big Town in favor of a more upscale enclosed mall at Northwest Highway and Central Expressway.

The annual Cotton Bowl parade on New Year's Day, 1962 fills Commerce Street with flags, floats, twirlers, and marching bands. At the end of the day, University of Texas fans would still be celebrating after the Longhorns beat the Rebels of Ole Miss by five points in front of a nationwide television audience.

Downtown lunch counters at Woolworth's, Sears, Kress, and Sanger's were off-limits to nonwhite customers before 1960 (although some stores, such as H. L. Green department store, had out-of-the-way counters for black patrons). Protesting with signs and rallies called attention to the inequity, but color barriers did not begin to fall until April of 1960, when two black theology students from SMU sat down at the whites-only counter in H. L. Green and refused to leave until they were served.

The Cotton Bowl has seen halftime performances by an estimated 3,000 different school marching bands since it opened in 1932, but few bands were showier than this group in about 1961.

In the 1960s, local television news departments took a larger role in covering national news, with local broadcast coverage of national elections, space shots, and a presidential inauguration. KRLD-TV's new "Studio A" provided additional room for increased coverage of news, sports, and weather.

Dallas's Theater Row shows some changes in this 1963 photo. The Majestic and Tower theaters still beckon moviegoers, but the Melba, closed for much of 1959, reopened as the Capri. The Capri was equipped to show super-widescreen Cinerama movies (such as *How the West Was Won*) but, due to lack of available Cinerama films, was often forced to erect a smaller screen at the front of the auditorium to show standard movies.

By Opening Day, 1963, the Dallas Eagles had merged with the Fort Worth Cats to become the Dallas–Fort Worth Rangers, playing AAA baseball in the Pacific Coast League as a farm club of the Minnesota Twins. Jack McKeon managed the 1963 Rangers, and the minor league team finally reached .500 for the season.

One of Dallas's first out-of-downtown luxury hotels was the Cabana Motor Hotel, which opened on the new Stemmons Freeway (between Slocum and Continental streets) in 1963. Outdoor fountains and colored lights attracted the attention of local drivers, and the hotel's Lanai Club featured Vegas-style shows and entertainment. (The Beatles would stay at the Cabana when visiting Dallas in 1966.)

Earlier showers had drifted away and the sky was cloudless on November 22, 1963, when President and Mrs.
John F. Kennedy arrived at Love Field in Air Force One. He was scheduled to speak at a luncheon at the Dallas
Trade Mart before flying to Houston that evening. Mrs. Kennedy holds a dozen Texas roses given to her by
a supporter; President Kennedy greets the airport crowd before the couple enters his limousine for a parade
through downtown Dallas.

Despite ugly incidents involving Lyndon Johnson in 1960 and an assault on U.N. ambassador Adlai Stevenson in Dallas several months before, the Dallas crowd reacted warmly and enthusiastically to the young president and his wife. The motorcade is westbound on Main Street, nearing the end of the parade route.

Texas governor John Connally and his wife are riding in the limousine with President and Mrs. Kennedy. "You certainly can't say Dallas doesn't love you," Nellie Connally told the president as their car pressed through crowds of adoring spectators.

The presidential limousine had just turned onto Elm Street (the curving street, left), when assassin Lee Harvey Oswald opened fire on the president from the sixth floor of the Texas School Book Depository with a cheap sniper rifle. The Hertz clock atop the depository building marked the time of the shots as 12:30 P.M.

Immediately after the shots, the president's limousine accelerated out of the area, leaving stunned bystanders and newsmen to make sense of the gunfire and carnage they just witnessed. Dallas clothing manufacturer Abraham Zapruder, standing just out of frame on the white pergola at left, took the most dramatic photos of the assassination with his home movie camera.

Still unsure as to who fired the shots or where they were fired from, Dallas police blockade the intersection of Elm and Houston streets and begin a search of the School Book Depository building. Meanwhile, Lee Harvey Oswald was making his escape from downtown Dallas to his Oak Cliff rooming house via bus and taxi.

At the emergency room entrance to Parkland Hospital, medical staff, media, police, and other onlookers await word on the condition of the president. Kennedy was declared dead from gunshot wounds at 1:00 P.M. Fearing a wider plot, Secret Service agents transported Vice-president Lyndon Johnson back to Love Field and to the security of *Air Force One*.

Federal judge Sarah T. Hughes administers the oath of office to now-President Lyndon Baines Johnson in a crowded compartment of *Air Force One*. Johnson's wife and President Kennedy's stricken widow stand at his sides. This photograph and a Dictabelt sound recording (its microphone is below Johnson's right elbow) provide the only record of the swearing-in ceremony.

Captured hours after shooting President Kennedy, assassin Lee Harvey Oswald was shot to death on national television by Dallas nightclub owner Jack Ruby (center rear). Humiliated by the double murders, Dallas officials wasted no time bringing Ruby to trial. Ruby was convicted of murder on March 14, 1964, but won an appeal for a new trial. Arrangements were under way for the trial when Ruby died of cancer.

Ford Motor Company's Dallas Assembly Plant churned out more than 94,000 vehicles during the 1964 production year, but a bitter strike as the plant geared up for its '65 model year shut down production for three weeks. The strike over pay and safety issues benched 1,450 Dallas workers.

Following Spread: Dallas Independent School District band students rehearse for a regional marching band competition in 1964. Dallas's growing suburban population required the district to build and open 37 new schools between 1956 and 1966.

Dallas Love Field (pictured) won a major victory in April 1964 when the Civil Aeronautics Board failed to designate Greater Southwest International Airport as the area's regional airport. Love Field celebrated by announcing plans to build two new parallel runways and double-deck the parking lot. The airport rivalry would be settled in the mid-1970s when the two cities cooperated on building DFW International Airport.

Veteran jazz trumpeter and vocalist Louis Armstrong visited Dallas in 1964 with his All-Star Band, featuring veteran jazzmen Danny Barcelona, Buster Bailey, Coleman Hawkins, and others. At the time, Dallas nightclubs and other entertainment venues were attracting a glittering roster of national acts.

Three of Dallas's newest downtown buildings jut into the twilit sky in this 1965 photo. From left to right are the Southland Life Building (completed in 1958), Republic National Bank Tower (1964), and First National Bank Building (1965).

The movie houses of Theater Row on Elm Street in 1965 were finding it hard to compete with newer theaters springing up in the suburbs. The Majestic and Tower theaters would seek to book major roadshow engagements while the Capri alternated exploitation movies with any available Cinerama movies.

Dallas's traditionally black Trinity Lodge of the Benevolent and Protective Order of the Elks boasted an 80-year history of community service and charity. For Dallas's 1965 Independence Day parade, Trinity Lodge was selected to lead the contingent of Elks, then in Dallas for the national Grand Lodge convention. Trinity Lodge members are followed by the Pyle School marching band of Kaufman.

Protests against racial violence across the South spurred this march for racial equality in Dallas in 1965. Three thousand strong, the civil rights protesters—black and white together—assembled at Good Street Baptist Church on Good-Latimer Street for the march across Dallas to a rally at Ferris Plaza.

The Dallas Municipal Building on Commerce Street was a Beaux-Arts–style classic dating from 1914, but by 1964, it was far too small for the burgeoning affairs of a city on the national stage. City Council appointed a committee to consider where a new city hall could be built. The committee studied 13 locations, but recommended a 12-block site near Dallas Memorial Auditorium bounded by Akard, Canton, Ervay, and Marilla streets.

A group of avid golfers playing out of a rented locker room near Lemmon and Oak Lawn avenues chartered the
Dallas Golf and Country Club in 1897. By the time this clubhouse was completed in 1913, Dallas Country
Club had become a center of social activity for prominent Dallasites.

The Stage Door Restaurant was one of the few authentic full-service Dallas delicatessens when it opened on Elm Street (between Ervay and Live Oak streets) in 1965. Touted as "the home of lox and bagels," Stage Door served a varied crowd of businesspeople, shoppers, and theatergoers. Late-nighters could dine in the Playbill Room until 2 A.M., then take home fresh pastries produced at the Stage Door's bakery.

Titche-Goettinger (shown here), Neiman Marcus, J. C. Penney, and F. W. Woolworths were anchor tenants of the new NorthPark Shopping Center when it opened in 1965 at the intersection of Northwest Highway and Central Expressway. Visitors were struck by the sheer scale of the mall, the opulence of the decor, and management's attention to the finest details.

Moderate weather nine months out of the year and plenty of available land helped make golf a popular weekend sport among Dallas's growing population of young executives. City parks director L. B. Houston announced in 1965 plans for another municipal golf course to be located near Royal Lane and the Elm Fork of the Trinity River. Completed in 1968, the new course would be named for Houston.

Dallas was still looking for a major league baseball franchise in 1965, when the city of Arlington built Turnpike Stadium for the Dallas–Fort Worth Spurs. The 10,000-seat stadium was decidedly minor league, but a stadium expansion to 20,000 seats in 1970 allowed the Spurs to set attendance records. With the move to Dallas by the Washington Senators (as "Texas Rangers") in 1972, Dallas finally had its major league ball club.

The west end of Dallas received a needed burst of redevelopment energy in the mid-1960s with construction of Courthouse Plaza and the new Dallas County Courthouse at 600 Commerce Street (shown here on the far horizon, looking west from about Elm and Field streets).

Clad in their red, white, and blue outfits, the Kilgore Junior College Rangerettes and Kilgore band perform to a Tijuana Brass tune during halftime at the 1967 Cotton Bowl New Year classic. This was the eighteenth consecutive Cotton Bowl appearance for the nation's best-known collegiate drill team.

Waders, sunbathers, sailors, and Sunday drivers enjoy a rare wintertime warm spell at White Rock Lake in January 1967. As is typical for Dallas, the temperature dropped to below freezing the next evening.

Wisconsin equestrienne Elaine
Kramer demonstrates Roman-style
riding outside Fair Park Coliseum.
Kramer and her sorrels were in
Dallas for performances at the
eight-day Dallas All-Star Rodeo in
1967.

The National Beauty Academy was just one of many businesses responsible for propagating the "Dallas look" in hair, makeup, and apparel fashion during the 1960s. Here student stylists sign up at National's booth at the State Fair of Texas.

In this 1968 aerial view of downtown Dallas, looking north from above the I-35/I-30 junction, new buildings have altered the Dallas skyline. Southland Center, the second Republic National Bank Tower, LTV Tower, National Bank of Commerce Building, and First National Bank Tower have all been completed in the previous ten years. One Main Place is under construction (far left).

Organized as an NFL expansion team in 1960, the Dallas Cowboys went from a winless first season to winning several division championships under head coach Tom Landry by the middle of the decade. This is a 1968 pre-season game against cross-state rival Houston Oilers.

133

John Neely Bryan's log home, which generations of schoolchildren were told was the first built in Dallas, had to find a new home of its own in 1968 when it was displaced from the corner of Main and Houston streets for construction of an underground parking garage. The newspaper column about the move set off a tug-of-war between city and county officials over ownership of the old structure.

Bishop College students make a solemn march across campus to the Carr P. Collins Chapel for a memorial service honoring the recently slain Dr. Martin Luther King, Jr., in 1968. Dr. Milton K. Curry, president of the historically all-black college, presided over the service, consisting largely of songs from the civil rights era.

"Go Cowboys" takes on another meaning in 1968 when the team announces it is leaving Dallas's Cotton Bowl to build a new stadium in the suburban city of Irving. The stadium decision unleashed legions of "Boobirds," who also expressed their displeasure with quarterbacks Don Meredith and Craig Morton. By that year, however, the Cowboys were on their way to becoming "America's Team."

For a payment of just 15 cents, the new North Dallas Tollway in 1968 allowed faster access to downtown Dallas from the northern suburbs. (The south end of the tollway is in the foreground.) Initially, the tollway was open only as far north as Mockingbird Lane, but within a year, it extended to Loop 635 (LBJ Freeway).

One Main Place celebrates its first Christmas in 1968 with outdoor lighting and caroling by a 1,000-member girl's choir assembled from Dallas-area high schools. Filling a city block surrounded by Main, Elm, Field, and Griffin streets, One Main Place was intended to be part of a multi-building development.

In 1969 the Dallas Chamber of Commerce marked the beginning of the holiday shopping season with a giant balloon parade. This inflated elephant, Charlie Brown, Snoopy, a giant turkey, and a dozen other balloon figures floated down Elm Street, followed by Santa Claus on a fire truck.

Heather Burnett, shown here on the stand overlooking McCree Park Pool in 1969, was one of the first female lifeguards hired by the Dallas Parks Department for the city's public swimming pools. A fiery note to the parks department by the 16-year-old protested the city's discriminatory hiring practices and resulted in her being hired for one of the 90 summer lifeguard jobs.

Mrs. Neil Sanders was also breaking gender barriers when she was hired as the city's first female school safety patrolman. Shown here escorting North Lake Elementary students across the street, Mrs. Sanders said she had been trying to talk the police department into hiring her for the job for several years.

Thirty-four black students entered SMU's administrative building in 1969, vowing to stay until the university acceded to their demands for increased cultural awareness in the curriculum. Hundreds more students staged an impromptu rally during the five-hour sit-in to express their support.

An F4A Crusader fighter jet crashed at takeoff near the north end of the Dallas Naval Air Station in 1969, killing the pilot and causing extensive fire damage. The jet was designed and built by LTV Aerospace, one of many Dallas companies providing logistics support and materiel in support of the war in Vietnam by the end of the decade.

Dallas's rail lines are increasingly extraneous to the city's transportation and growth, and the area surrounding Dallas Memorial Auditorium is being prepared for construction of a larger convention center complex.

144

Miss Texas (Dana Dowell of Longview) sits atop a float in the 1969 State Fair of Texas parade. Her float represented the Moon Year Exposition theme. Miss Texas was not the only royalty in the parade; amid the marching bands and motorcycle clowns were Miss Wool and Mohair and the Texas Shorthorn Lassie Queen.

THE 1970s: THE DALLAS OF DALLAS

When opening credits for the new CBS miniseries *Dallas* first appeared in April 1978, Dallas was well on its way to becoming the seventh largest city in the nation. The long, low opening helicopter shot that made the city seem to appear from nowhere shows off a spiky skyline that was 30 years in the making. And when the same helicopter camera peeped down through the roof into Texas Stadium, the Dallas Cowboys had already won two Super Bowls and five conference championships.

Dallas, the television series, didn't invent Dallas, the city. Instead, it reflected the wealth, glamour, style, and drama that Dallas had developed in the previous decades.

The city had forsaken the cotton trading markets in the 1950s; by the 1970s, Dallas was making its money in oil, real estate, insurance, finance, and technology. The Dallas Market Center complex was drawing up to 50,000 retailers to town a month, dominating wholesale markets for apparel, furniture, giftware, and accessories. Developers continued to remodel the skyline with tall buildings: Bryan Tower, the Campbell Center buildings, One Dallas Centre, and Renaissance Tower (which is, coincidentally, home to the fictional Ewing Oil). Union Depot still welcomed the occasional passenger train, but Dallas–Fort Worth International Airport was spread over more acreage than Manhattan Island and (depending on how you measured) was the world's busiest passenger airport. The Dallas Cowboys Cheerleaders were traveling the world, exporting a made-in-Dallas style combining jiggle, a healthy tan, and well-applied makeup.

Dallas created its own superlatives before *Dallas* shared them with the world.

Within two years, 30 million people a week were seeing the Dallas of *Dallas,* but there were things about the city that a viewer would never see. They didn't see the State Fair of Texas, where a family could spend a pleasant day together without need of liquor or firearms. And they wouldn't know that a full acre of prime downtown real estate was set aside for the sole purpose of quiet reflection and thanksgiving.

In the 1970s, the city was the Dallas of *Dallas.* And more.

The anger and protests and sit-ins of the 1960s led to a different type of event in Dallas's Lee Park in 1970. Two thousand young people in ponchos, jeans, and beads gathered under the columns of Arlington Hall for a non-denominational Jesus Rally.

Iconic Dallas Cowboys head coach Tom Landry (wearing his trademark fedora) used modern engineering and quality-control techniques to steer his team to a record-setting 20 consecutive winning seasons. Two Super Bowl victories and the move to the $1.15 billion Texas Stadium earned Landry and the Cowboys international recognition in the 1970s. Linebacker Lee Roy Johnson can be seen standing behind Landry.

Dallas's growing population of the 1960s and 1970s most often found homes in communities sprouting from cotton fields in the city's northern suburbs. But stately homes such as this one, located on the meandering banks of Turtle Creek, were prized by the wealthy.

Girls on horseback listen to a free Labor Day weekend concert by the Dallas Symphony Orchestra at Flagpole Hill. When rain showers threatened, the audience—livestock included—moved under the park shelter with orchestra members.

A Weatherford farm boy sells 100-pound "Cobb Gem" watermelons from his family's stall at Dallas Farmers Market. A bountiful local melon crop in 1970 brought the price of cantaloupes down to $2.50 a bushel and watermelons to four cents a pound that season.

152

Almost seven years after the assassination, Dallas dedicates the John F. Kennedy Memorial near
Courthouse Plaza on June 24, 1970. Designed by architect Phillip Johnson as a cenotaph (empty tomb),
the austere 50-foot-by-50-foot box-like structure is open to the sky and identified only by a black marble
slab with the inscription, "John F. Kennedy."

Dallas families could view exotic wildlife without ever leaving the air-conditioned comfort of their cars when World of Animals opened in 1970 off Lawson Road near Highway 20 in Mesquite. Rhinos, elephants, zebras, chimps, gibbons, and 500 other species of wild animals roamed free while tourists locked in their cars drove through the wildlife preserve.

Families enjoy a spring afternoon at historic Kidd Springs Park in Oak Cliff. Originally a private park for boating and fishing, Kidd Springs was acquired by the city following WWII.

The Jeep-mounted First Cavalry Division band from Fort Hood leads the 1971 Fourth of July
parade past the reviewing stand at the Baker Hotel (right). The parade had a decidedly martial feel
with military marching bands, drill teams, patriotic organizations, and a float depicting imprisoned
POWs in Vietnam.

Students at Benito Juarez Elementary School, located in one of the more dismal patches of West Dallas, celebrate the last day of the school year in 1972. Construction to replace the dilapidated buildings was delayed by federal lawsuits, but protests by parents' groups eventually resulted in closure of the 50-year-old school.

Two boys try out the sandbox at Caruth Park following the addition of some new unique play equipment. Buried telephone poles, industrial piping, railroad ties, and concrete sewer pipe combined into tunnels and mazes made the park a great place for exploration and unstructured play.

In 1972, 400 students rally on the SMU campus in support of 21 students evicted from a building they had occupied to protest bombing raids of North Vietnam. Two protesters were injured when armed campus security officers removed the group from the building.

Following Spread: The second running of the White Rock Marathon attracted 144 runners from 15 states and resulted in a winning time of two hours, 43 minutes. Sponsored by the Dallas Cross Country Club, the marathon treated entrants to a tour of Dr. Kenneth Cooper's new Aerobics Center and a carbo-loading meal at the Majestic Steak House.

Another new drive-through wildlife park came to the area when Lion Country Safari opened in 1972. The 485-acre wildlife park featured an 85-acre entertainment complex, which included a miniature railroad, a petting zoo, bird shows, and a riverboat ride. Lion Country became another of the tourist attractions clustered along the highway between Dallas and Fort Worth.

Even as workers cleared the wreckage of a small plane off its runway in 1972, Red Bird Airport in South Dallas was approved by the Texas Aeronautics Commission for commuter service to the new Dallas–Fort Worth International Airport. Metroflight Airlines of Dallas planned to operate helicopter and STOL service from Red Bird to the new regional airport.

Except for this float reenacting the famous WWII flag-raising on Iwo Jima, the 1972 Fourth of July parade in downtown Dallas was decidedly less militaristic and more celebratory than the 1971 parade. Flag-waving Boy Scouts, Camp Fire girls, Shriners, zebras from the World of Animals, and the Dallasettes baton corps marched down Main Street and south on Akard Street to Memorial Auditorium.

Designated hitter Alex Johnson of the Texas Rangers slides into home plate during an afternoon game at Ranger Stadium. Despite Johnson's .287 batting average, the 1973 season was another in a long line of losing seasons for the Rangers, who finished sixth in the American League West.

Mexican-Americans gather at the Dallas Municipal Building demanding answers about the death of 11-year-old Santo Rodriguez. The boy was detained for questioning by two Dallas police officers before being shot in the head and killed while sitting in the patrol car. A Dallas police officer was eventually found guilty of Rodriguez's murder.

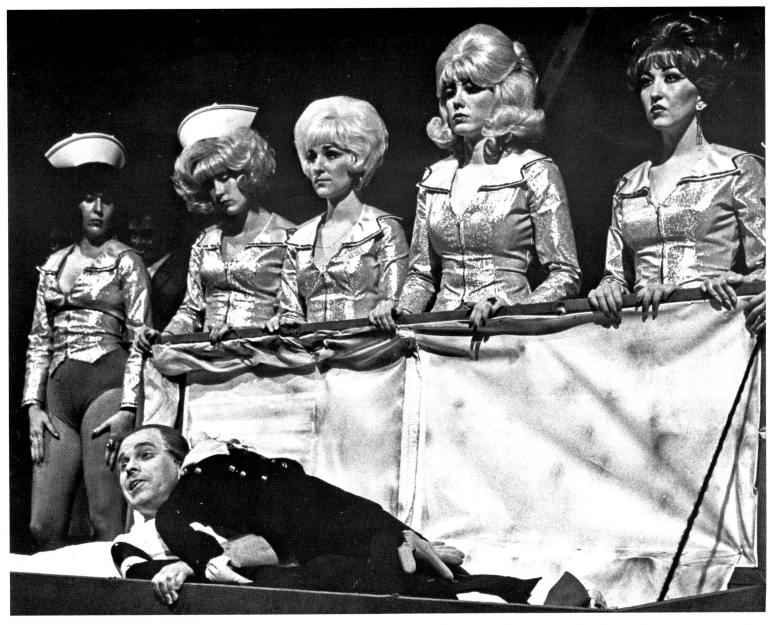

One of Dallas's most notorious characters (in the person of veteran actor Ken Latimer) appeared onstage when *Jack Ruby, All-American Boy* debuted at the Dallas Theater Center in 1974. The play told the story of the city's darkest days through the mind of the strip club operator who shot Lee Harvey Oswald.

By 1974, Dallas's agricultural heritage was as foreign to most of the increasingly cosmopolitan population as this steam tractor is to the girls who are staring at it. By the 1970s, fewer than one in 15 Dallasites had ever earned their living on a farm.

High winter clouds whisk across Dallas skies in this 1975 photo taken from southwest of downtown.

A couple admires the high-rise residences and the 18-story Turtle Creek Village building that line tree-shaded Turtle Creek. By 1975, tall office buildings were erected or under construction throughout much of North Dallas.

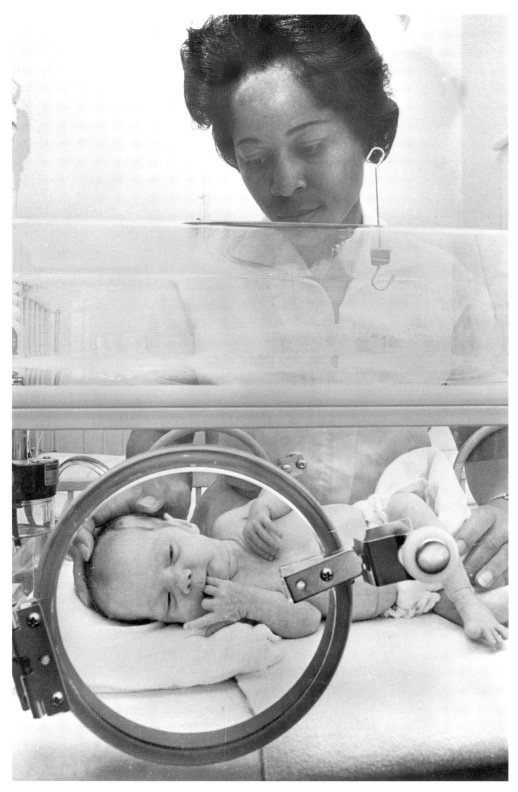

A nurse tends to a baby brought to the Children's Medical Center in one of the new emergency transport devices in 1975. The Metropolitan Dallas Chapter of the March of Dimes equipped Dallas fire stations and paramedic units with these infant incubators to assist in the transfer of critically ill babies to the nearest care center.

Construction workers at Dallas–Fort Worth International Airport uncovered the bones of a 90-million-year-old swimming dinosaur, shown here being restored under the direction of Bob H. Slaughter, director of vertebrate paleontology at SMU. Braniff International Airlines offered to underwrite restoration costs in return for the opportunity to display the skeleton at their D-FW Airport terminal.

An impromptu Cinco de Mayo parade of elementary school students and others from the "Little Mexico" community form around the Pinkston High School ROTC drill team for the march to Pikes Park in 1975. "Little Mexico," located just north of downtown Dallas, was home to thousands of Mexican-American families and businesses.

The Texas Rangers continued to draw good crowds for so-so seasons. Coach Billy Martin, called "Baseball's Fiery Genius" by *Sports Illustrated*, was fired mid-season in 1975 after a 44-51 start.

Robert E. Lee and his aide get a rare dusting of snow. The lifesize statue of the mounted Civil War general, erected in Lee Park by the Dallas Southern Memorial Association after an eight-year fundraising effort, was unveiled by President Franklin D. Roosevelt in a special ceremony at the park in 1936.

Crowds found every available vantage point (including this parking lot on Commerce Street) to view the nationally telecast 1976 Cotton Bowl parade. Television hosts Sally Struthers, William Conrad, and Larry Linville introduced more than 30 decorated floats, 12 college marching bands, and hosts of equestrian teams. The Arkansas Razorbacks met the Georgia Bulldogs in the Cotton Bowl later than afternoon.

177

A group waits out a brief rain shower at a city intersection. Downtown Dallas was no longer
the retail shoppers' destination that it had been 20 years before; by 1976 the weekday sidewalks
were filled mostly with businesspeople, tourists, and service workers.

Students eye each other warily on the first day of school in the L. G. Pinkston High School cafeteria. A court-ordered school desegregation plan implemented in 1976 sent some students far from their neighborhoods to attend new schools.

It may be Independence Day, but it's still a work day for Tim Rhys as he delivers Dr. Pepper from his flag-decorated truck. On the Fourth of July in 1976, the U.S. bicentennial year, Dallas was awash in red, white, and blue.

Ten-year-old Junior Jones looks up at one of the cast bells ready for installation in Thanks-Giving Square, a new park at the corner of Pacific Avenue and Ervay Street. This 4,600-pound "C" bell was one of three in the park's bell tower, all cast in the shape of the Liberty Bell. Thanks-Giving Square was dedicated in 1976 to promote the universal concept of giving thanks.

The 20-story Medical Arts Building, erected in 1923 on Pacific Avenue at Ervay Street, tasted the wrecking ball in 1977. Home to medical practitioners for more than 50 years (and claimed to be the city's first medical center), the Medical Arts Building no longer complied with new Dallas fire codes for tall buildings.

Tenants gather in the Hall of Nations for dedication of the new World Trade Center, the sixth building in the Dallas Market Center complex on Stemmons Freeway. Completion of the 1.4 million-square-foot building made the Dallas Market Center the world's largest single-site wholesale merchandising complex and reinforced Dallas's reputation as a world center for fashion, decor, and design.

Another spring weekend at White Rock Lake Park means another day for picnics, sunbathing, guitars, Frisbees, and horseback riding. Improvements to the parkland surrounding the lake in the 1970s provided more space for outdoor entertainment.

Like a scene from an Alfred Hitchcock movie, birds swarm over Ferris Plaza near Houston and Wood streets. The migrating birds are attracted to the thick foliage of live oak trees in Ferris Plaza and nearby Dealey Plaza.

Spurred by memories of slain 11-year-old Santo Rodriguez and several 1977 incidents of police brutality in Texas, hundreds of Mexican-Americans marched through downtown Dallas in protest. The peaceful march began with a prayer service at the Kennedy Memorial and ended at Our Lady of Guadalupe Catholic Church (also known as the Cathedral Shrine of the Virgin of Guadalupe) at 2500 N. Harwood.

Walden Prep students enjoy a casual outdoor study session. Walden Preparatory School opened in North Dallas for students who could flourish in a less-structured academic setting.

Few buildings symbolized Dallas's entry onto an international stage more than the new Dallas City Hall, designed by renowned architect I. M. Pei. The first city council meeting was held there in 1978.

Dallas City Hall offices face International Plaza, which includes public meeting space, a reflecting pool, and fountains. Architect I. M. Pei's horizontal design and inverted pyramid shape contrasts with the more vertical design of Dallas's rising skyline. Support for the cantilevered construction comes from the four massive cylinders.

Sculptor Henry Morgan, internationally known for his obsession with totemic objects and bone-line structures, was commissioned to create this piece of public art for installation outside the new Dallas City Hall.

Though she's shown here in the costume of "Minnie Pearl," her hillbilly persona, comic Sarah Cannon dressed in heels and tailored suit when she met Dallas investors to raise money for her chain of chicken restaurants. By the 1970s Dallas money was helping finance businesses around the world.

Firefighters lean out of the window of a fire-gutted residence at Rawlins and Douglas streets. Many of the city's older buildings—some dating back 75 years or more—were particularly vulnerable to fire.

A Dallas firefighter stands on top of a smoking building. As the city tightened rules for historic preservation, an increasing number of fires of suspicious origin consumed some of the city's older structures.

Fashion retailers Woolf Brothers (formerly Dreyfuss & Son), Volk Brothers, and others occupied the city block bounded by Main, Ervay, Elm, and St. Paul streets. (It's viewed here from Main Street, looking north on Ervay Street). Even as the retailers relocated to the suburbs in the late 1970s, plans were underway to level the block for construction of a 60-story banking building.

It's a slow day for produce at the Dallas Farmers Market. This farmer grabs a quick nap on the bed of his truck while waiting for customers. For many Dallasites, Farmers Market is their only link to the city's rural heritage.

196

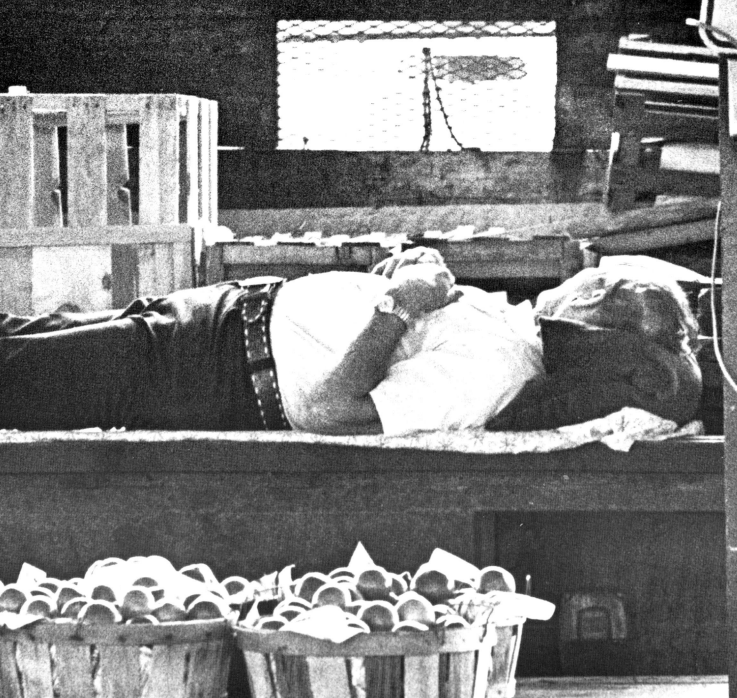

Though a city of the South, Dallas had little patience for the Ku Klux Klan. Following a 1978 shooting in North Carolina by Klansmen and the announcement of a Klan rally in Dallas, thousands of anti-Klan demonstrators flooded International Plaza. Riot police were called to separate anti-Klan demonstrators from members of the Klan. A similar rally in 1922 drew 5,000 anti-Klan protesters to downtown Dallas.

The venerable Kirby Building, located at Main and Akard streets, was threatened by redevelopment in 1974. Asked to place a freeze on demolition of several historic Dallas structures, the city council wavered, trying to find the proper balance between property rights and historical significance.

There's more than a century of Dallas progress in this single view. In the foreground is the pioneer cabin attributed to Dallas pioneer John Neeley Bryan. The Romanesque Revival building is "Old Red," which served as the Dallas County Courthouse for 75 years. The lighted ball and restaurant atop Reunion Tower is recognized worldwide from the opening credits of *Dallas.*

NOTES ON THE PHOTOGRAPHS

These notes, listed by page number, attempt to include all aspects known of the photographs. Each of the photographs is identified by the page number, photograph's title or description, photographer and collection, archive, and call or box number when applicable. Although every attempt was made to collect all data, in some cases complete data may have been unavailable due to the age and condition of some of the photographs and records.

II   REPUBLIC BANK AND MERCANTILE AND MAGNOLIA BUILDINGS
Dallas Public Library
PA76-1-17015-1

VI   CARNIVAL OF BOOKS
Dallas Public Library
PA87-1-61048

X   CENTRAL EXPRESSWAY
Dallas Public Library
PA2000-3-622

2   STATE FAIR MIDWAY
Dallas Public Library
PA76-1-412-2

3   MARIACHI BAND AND MKT PASSENGERS
Dallas Public Library
PA76-1-20385-5

4   POLICE AT MAIN AND HARWOOD
Dallas Public Library
PA76-1-939-3

5   A. HARRIS AND CO.
Dallas Public Library
PA2000-3-189

6   TRAFFIC IN SNOW
Dallas Public Library
PA76-1-9070-28

7   WALGREEN DRUGS IN SNOWSTORM
Dallas Public Library
PA76-1-5445

8   SMU FOOTBALL TEAM
Dallas Public Library
PA76-1-13335-4

9   GLITTERING ELM STREET
Dallas Public Library
PA76-1-576-2

10   VAN CAMP'S CANNERY
Dallas Public Library
PA76-1-9142-6

12   AUDIE MURPHY RODEO ARENA
Dallas Public Library
PA76-1-2895-2

13   MESQUITE
Dallas Public Library
PA76-1-1074-1

14   AIRPHIBIAN
Dallas Public Library
PA76-1-4238-1

15   TEXAS SPECIAL
Dallas Public Library
PA76-1-20384-4

16   PUBLIC POOL
Dallas Public Library
PA76-1-2702-2

17   RETAIL DISTRICT ON ELM
Dallas Public Library
PA76-1-14316-1

18   DALLAS COUNTRY CLUB EASTER EGG HUNT
Dallas Public Library
PA76-1-820-1

19   MAIN STREET FIRE
Dallas Public Library
PA76-1-5451-7

20   AKARD STREET CANYON
Dallas Public Library
PA76-1-20403-4

21   MAYOR THORNTON GREETS SENATOR LYNDON B. JOHNSON
Dallas Public Library
PA76-1-11698

22   GAINESVILLE COMMUNITY CIRCUS
Dallas Public Library
PA76-1-8006-1

23   BEN HOGAN
Dallas Public Library
PA76-1-9465-8

24   PRESIDENT EISENHOWER AND WIFE MAMIE
Dallas Public Library
PA76-1-11179-12

25   DALLAS EAGLES' DAVE HOSKINS
Dallas Public Library
PA76-1-9160-5

26   DALLAS EAGLES
Dallas Public Library
PA76-1-7998-2

27   DALLAS TEXANS
Dallas Public Library
PA76-1-10905-7

28   HOCKADAY SCHOOL ATHLETES
Dallas Public Library
PA76-1-2620

30   MOCK ATOMIC BOMB DRILL
Dallas Public Library
PA76-1-16502-2

31   1953 ARMED FORCES DAY PARADE
Dallas Public Library
PA76-1-12784-4

32   PLEASURE ISLAND CAST
Dallas Public Library
PA2001-7-20-7

33   THE "AIRPORT OF TOMORROW" GRAND OPENING
Dallas Public Library
PA76-1-13392-3

34   DALLAS FARMERS MARKET
Dallas Public Library
PA76-1-13129-2